SPINNING

CAUSE
MOMENTUM MATTERS

BY S. E. MCKENZIE

ISBN-10: 1928069819

DEDICATION
To everyone who has been left out in the cold

THIS BOOK IS A BOOK OF SPECULATIVE FICTION
Characters, companies, governments, places, events, are either
products of the author's imagination or used fictitiously. Any
resemblance to persons (living or dead), companies, governments,
places and/or events, is a coincidence and unintended.

TABLE OF CONTENTS

SPINNING

SPINning
I

I saw my dreams so out of reach;
Spinning in the sky;
I asked them why;

Then my dreams came tumbling down

And fell to the ground
Without a sound
Without a cry;

The snake
Was toyed with
By a sharp stick;

Outraged
It circled its prey
Though the prey tried to runaway.

The snake looked at me
And then looked at Ted
Who was counting his wealth left by Fred;

SPINning

Fred never met Ted;
The grandson born
Years after Fred was dead.

With a tear in his eye, the snake said,
"I have been so misunderstood
Day by day,"

Ted looked away
Not interested
In a word that snake had to say.

Ted went on counting his wealth;
Product of Fred's sacrifice and virtue;
And the freedom

That was still left;
Before Fred passed away.
Though no one had the time of day

To say goodbye;
Fred did not cry;
While the children played in the rain

They had nowhere else to go;

While toxic towns
Conditioned people
To stay guarded

While smiling sweetly;
Professional agitators
Held hands with social engineers;

And they all came around;
Stomping their feet on the ground
Commenting on our appearance

Stirring up fear;
Ruining the atmosphere
Whenever they were near.

And Fred once said,
"I will always spin with you,
Where ever I may be;

In the sun;
Where life must have begun;
Making us a derivative

SPINning

Of One.
Don't need
No sum zero games

No more;
In the place I will be
For evermore."

While the ragged people on earth
Stayed in rusty vans below their worth;
Parked on land

Out of sight
Of the Power Clique's
Might;

The rain turned to snow.
As the decay grew
Behind the fence

The Power Clique
Had erected;
The forgotten people shivered;

Left out in the cold
As they grew old;
The power Clique

Lied as the poor people died;
Victims of the growing decay
Accelerating day by day.

Ted no long lived
In the country of his descent;
That land was left far behind;

So proudly;
A long time ago.
Before the name change.

Now, the new land
Is developed
For rent;

II

And day by day; the ragged people
Behind the fence were forgotten;
While decay

SPINning

Made so much go rotten.

Culture of obstruction
And provocation;
Hot passion was no longer the fashion.

But you must never speak out loud;
For the Power Clique
Do not want to remember you;

As you really are;
The power Clique
Make war;

Not love;
For they are perpetually angry;
They watch but cannot see;

They bait
But cannot communicate
For they are living

In a killing machine;

Brought up to be mean;
So well dressed;
They laugh at the dispossessed;

So wrongly assessed;
How they love
To torment and oppress.

III

Channeled through heartlessness
We spin;
You touching me; we spin;

Holding on to our skin
We spin
We do not bleed

Or die in need;
We spin
To create

Momentum;
And one day
We will win

SPINning

The race
While keeping
Pace;

Avoiding the face
We see all over the place.
We walk with grace;

Down the path
We learn to love
You and me;

Each one of us;
We spin;
Through all this trouble;

We spin;
Through all this rubble;
We spin.

IV

After Ted builds his wall;
And leaves us far behind
We vow not to fall

S.E. McKENZIE

Nor be baited
By those
Who want us hated;

We will spin
Around one sun
Where life must have begun;

On this earth, we share her worth.

Love will show us how;
Give us enough strength
To spin;

We will build
The momentum;
We will let it begin;

From the disruption caused
As they watched but would not see
The disaster in motion

That they created
While they were insulated
From our pain;

SPINning

The children played out in the rain
They had nowhere else
To go;

And it was beginning to snow.

Traffic like a snake
Goes by so fast, never slow.
We know our world

Cannot last.
Careless as they see;
Careless as they speak;

Careless as they chart
The map
That creates our path.

We spin
Like dots on a scatterplot
Before the aftermath.

We spin to project our momentum;
We crawl under the wall;
No matter how tall;

First one out
Might spill
Their blood in the mud;

We are the forgotten ones.
Only in peace
Will we be free;

We refuse to be dispossessed
Underdressed
A victim to be oppressed;

Their crime can never be confessed;
Just hidden behind the fence;
As time flew by;

The Power Clique
Was so elated;
Happily living

In their world so petty and gated;

Cost of living was now inflated;
The devaluation had begun;
Under one sun;

SPINning

Drugs were piped into the water supply
Unintentionally;
Made many bloated and sedated;

Between rigid rules
That gave power to fools
A tree became uprooted

Leaving a hole wide open;
Into it a life was stolen
Found dead and frozen;

As the wind changed
Torrents flew by;
As Fred started to cry;

Water soaked into the ground;
But us;
Still had the might to be free

As the Power Clique
Grew their new
Social Order

They left us out in the cold
As we grew old;
Decay grew behind the fence.

Technology
Replaced
Many;

To fit into the new command
That was taking over the land
Controlling demand

The Power Clique tyrannized
With forced guardianship
Of the living;

Decay was unforgiving;

Growing at a rate
So individualized
Controlled by the Power Clique's force;

So collectivized;
The only way to be civilized;
The Power Clique said;

SPINning

"Only the crazy
Listen to their own voice
Buried in their head.

For there is only
One way;
Our way,"

The Power Clique said

While the decay grew;
And ate
Whoever stood in its path;

We were the victims
Of the aftermath;
Now many

Did not even have access to a bath.

As the Power Clique
Dominated
In their one-way world

That spread;
With the superhighway
Where cameras

Were everywhere
Taking multiple snaps
At the same time.

There was the right way
And the wrong way;
No room for common sense to linger;

The Power Clique knew how
To smile sweetly
As they killed;

But could no longer innovate;
Decay was in the air
And everywhere;

Grew day by day;

The Power Clique were so out of touch,
For their power was able to insulate
Them; so sheltered from the reality of others;

How they laughed
As they grew richer
And the poor grew poorer;

SPINning

The Power Clique had Monopoly Power
To cause prices
To inflate

For their friends;
Were always ready
To make amends;

It was true;
Our future was in decline;
The thought of it

Could burn out your mind;
Negativity was the Power Clique's tool;
Toxic Energy;

To not question it
Made you a fool;
While the Power Clique watched

They could not see the process so cruel;

For they had grown to be
Too
Willfully blind.

Behind the wall;
No longer seen
As neighbors;

Sisters and brothers
Living inside a living universe
Which some said cared;

And shared its bounty;
Adding value
Day by day;

While the Power Clique
Told us to go away
And not be seen;

The world that we knew
Was getting mean
Some tried to destroy our self-esteem

Tried to drive us to suicide.

During the careless days
Where they watched in a daze;
But could not see.

SPINning

Made them so proud out loud;
For they controlled fate
Could create the power to insulate.

The children cried all night;
Left alone in a place Fred had built
Many years ago;

Some just had
Enough money
To pay the rent;

So
They no longer
Had to live in a tent;

The snake
Was never welcome
In any neighborhood;

Every door has been closed
By the Power Clique;
How can the meek

S.E. McKENZIE

Inherit anything?"
The snake said
Years after Fred was dead;

To succeed
You must be
Opportunistic

Holding on
While the world is spinning all around;
Holding on to your ground

While you are still winning.
I am full of life
And I have seen

Many fooled by their sadness;

Too many victims
With broken dreams
That were never lived;

For life is a circle;
Spinning around;
Left in a cruel world

SPINning

Where you never belong;
Stuck behind the fence
There is little opportunity

While Ghetto Queen
Loves to tease
With her wealth;

Loves to break promises
Creating anger;
Her tool so cruel;

Designed to burn out the mind.
Some would be
Caught in the trap

And would lose their sense
Of harmony
Stunted for evermore;

Not able to grow to be
What could have been
Before;

V

The best you could be;
Your full potential;
To gain a credential;

Decay grew faster;
As the Power Clique laughed
At what they had done;

Their gated world
Now had more sun
While ours was covered in shadow

And sorrow;

So stagnant; could not grow nor progress
While today was turning into tomorrow;
The world was spinning too fast;

Its ground
Stomped upon
By the mechanical pig;

Leaving bones
All alone
In a hole

SPINning

Dug with a heart of stone.

The warhead
Was flying and crying
In the sky;

A tool for a fool;
The mean
Have monopolistic rule

Hiding their roots
Buried so deep
In the ground;

Hoping Truth had lied.

Lost in forgotten memories
That thrived
Decades ago.

Silently died
Without a sound; after Fred's
Heart could no longer pound.

You must not speak

Of the unseen;
Steely Beast;
So cruel

Under the sea
Living
In a rusty submarine.

VI
Cult of fear
Designed by
The nouveau

Social Engineer
Was always near
We spin to avoid what we fear;

We are a moving dot
On a scatter plot;
As we spin

Momentum
Creates
All we've got;

SPINning

We spin
To avoid
What we fear;

We spin
As we take flight;
We spin

To avoid a fight

With Ghetto Queen
Creeping around
Controlling her ground

Destroying any chance
To relate;
How she loves to bait;

Looking for prey;
We are out of sight
We spin

As one into the night;
Waiting for the morning light;
To hold us in Nature's warmth.

VII

The monolithic
Mechanical Pig;
Watches but cannot see;

Hears but cannot listen;
Fear loops around his mind;
Sadistic; simplistic; unkind;

Nothing of value to sell
Except the knowledge
To engineer fear;

No space for Common Sense to linger
While Ghetto Queen
Has you wrapped around her finger;

So able to manufacture consent;
So unable to invent;
How she loves to torment;

"If you don't do exactly as I say;
I will psychologically
Damage

SPINning

She says with a sneer.
We no long live
In the country of our descent;

I will decide the cost of your rent;
I am the one
In charge of consent;"

Ghetto Queen
Looks so cool
With her hannah red hair;

If you don't fear her
You will soon be turned into
A tool for a fool;

She throws out insults
To control our space;
The place where we hide

Our face.
Still, we walk in grace
Under one sun.

Ghetto Queen
Is so overdressed;
She is so elite

And she loves to oppress;
We know we should not speak;
Act as if we are not there;

For she can only share her hate;
Loves to bait;
Doesn't try to communicate;

And she holds
The power of the flame
How she loves to inflame

Our fear;
To lose ourselves;
In the fear she loves to spread;

SPINning

She looks at us
We know
She wants us dead.

VIII
She whispers at you
As you leave the bank
So proud to remind you

Of your rank;
Ghetto Queen owns it all;
No room for market correction;

Only the Ghetto Queen
Has to the power
Of selection;

How she loves to control
With her Negative
Suggestion;

We hear the Ghostly voice say
"For thirty years
I had to pay triple net

S.E. McKENZIE

And what did I get;
When I was too old to work
They took all I had

Then just let me die;"

Public space; no longer free;
Loss of Privacy;
We fight for our sanity;

Us; Ragged People;
Too weary to take
Another step

Ghetto Queen;
So mean; would destroy
All your tomorrows;

While crushing your dream.

Baiter; hater;
Instigator;
Inflator;

Of the cost of living

SPINning

In a rat hole gets steeper;
She gets her way;
Every day;

Enjoying her pay day
Making Ragged People's life
Hell;

Making it harder to buy
Instead of increasing
The market supply.

IX

Spinning around
With feet firmly on the ground;
Not allowed to speak

Cannot make a sound
We are too weak;
We spin

To create momentum
To surround us
While the test

Is in motion;

Cannot rest;
When the day comes
A new name is given to you;

If you complain;
Ghetto Queen will show distain
Cause you pain

For the billing code
Is the new bible that must be followed
Without a grumble

Lie down now
While you worry about your sanity
While others say

You have been lost in depravity;
Keep your eyes on the road
See the new car

Paid by the billing code
See the advertisement
On the license plate;

SPINning

Run out of the door
Before
It is too late.

The meeting
Does not include you
So they will never know

The facts
That made
Who you are, true.

X

Looking for something to live for
In a world
Dominated by war;

News that made you
Feel so bad;
Helps you forget

How much you can't have
Which could have changed your life;
So the world could grow to be

S.E. McKENZIE

Less sad.

Seen too much
From the baiter who loves to hate;
Seen too much behind the barrier

Which limits our fate;
Slows down momentum;
As our energy is captured

And frozen in time.

Even more energy is captures
Through the Public Internet Carrier
Following our every move;

Captures images of our faces too;
On cameras
Snapping shots

All at the same time.

XI
Mean Girls
Here and there
Putting on make-up;

SPINning

Doing their hair;
Sexualize who they want
As if the other person

Is not there;
Drives some to suicide
As they take over space

After they brush on
A different face;
A new look;

For Facebook.

XII

Nouveau Gestapo's sneer;
The first step
In a campaign of smear;

Demoralized for pay
And a stay
In a private resort;

On Christmas Day
Mean Girl
And the watchers stand all around;

Looking at homeless people who are down;
"You look like a recovering alci,
Here is a bottle of wine;"

How Ghetto Queen laughs
As she walks by the ragged people;
Wearing their Goodwill clothes;

Just garbage to some;
She whispers;
An insult in someone's ear;

The ragged person
Responds in fear
As Ghetto Queen laughs

Ragged Person is now sucked into her game;

Now the ragged person will be
The one to blame;
The Ghetto Queen

SPINning

So well fed;
She smiles so sweetly;
After she adds insult to injury;

The feeling of fear is now so near;

Ghetto Queen's life goes on the same;
Loving the power to insult after injury;
Gives her a feeling of joy;

For other people's
Emotions
Are just her toy;

Only Ghetto Queen can win;
Nouveau Gestapo drives by
And says "hi,

Why don't you make them cry;
Make them wanna die,
If they disappear

Our beautification project
Will be closer to complete
And then we will enjoy

What it means to be elite."
Ghetto Queen nods;
As she holds on

To her Poinsettia tightly;
Just slightly toxic;
If a pet does ingest

Consultation fees
May apply;
Ghetto Queen

Holds life and death
In her hands;
She feels so mighty;

Manipulator of emotions so deep
Better to let
Sleep.

XIII

Threatening an assault
Is never a tort
For the Mechanical Pig;

SPINning

As the Ghetto Queen
Spins her hype
Shaping a biased stereotype;

Once a year.
The revolving door
Lets a few out.

Now broken and torn and worn;
The list for everything
Channels the dispossessed

Through identifiable labels
Often misused
And abused;

Labels to disconnect
From those
Whose status depends

On being over-dressed;

Money; quantified power to control one's fate;
If only for a moment;
Before cost of living

Spirals out of control
After oil markets crash;
We all wait for the next boom;

The flags are waving;
We are told
We are heading for doom;

That we are misbehaving by living.

In a program of beautification
The ghetto queen loves making a scene
To show her superior position

To us;
It was Tyranny
That we tried to resist;

She drove right into us
But missed;
We said something to a passerby

SPINning

But she put her nose up in the air;
Acted as if we weren't there;
Confirmed how the Power Clique is everywhere;

Process of bad decision making
By others who do not care;
Leads to despair;

And to disparity so unfair;

Fabricating negative suggestion;
No time to question;
Too much rush

In all this congestion.
The war generation
Played it like a game;

So collectivized
And dehumanized
No curiosity

Left.

No positive imagination spent;
We lived in a world
Of manufactured consent;

No relationships forming;
Just Control Gangs swarming.
Some said it was the end of the world

And were making it so;

And love had so far to go;
For all was now controlled
No room

For common sense to grow;
As today flowed into tomorrow;
We could not sleep;

We were too cold;
Growing old;
Many were shifting

Into an impersonal role;

SPINning

As the Power Clique's domain
Was just a place of pain;
Where decay

Turned everything into rot;
While Ghetto Queen
Looked into the mirror,

And then painted her face again.

THE END

Produced by S.E. McKenzie Productions
First Print Edition December 2015

Enquiries: 1(778)992-2453
Mailing Address:
S. E. McKenzie Productions
168 B 5ᵗʰ St.
Courtenay, BC
V9N 1J4

Email Address:
messidartha@aol.com

http://www.amazon.com/SarahMcKenzie/e/B00H9RWX48/